Celticology Trivia Challenge

Boston Celtics Basketball

Celticology Trivia Challenge – Boston Celtics Basketball;
First Edition 2008

Published by
Kick The Ball, Ltd
8595 Columbus Pike, Suite 197
Lewis Center, OH 43035
www.TriviaGameBooks.com

Designed, Formatted, and Edited by: Paul F. Wilson & Tom P. Rippey III
Researched by: Ann E. Wilson

International Standard Book Number: 978-1-934372-53-1

Printed & Bound in the United States of America

Paul F. Wilson & Tom P. Rippey III

Celticology Trivia Challenge

Boston Celtics Basketball

Researched by Ann E. Wilson

Paul F. Wilson & Tom P. Rippey III, Editors

Kick The Ball, Ltd
Lewis Center, Ohio

This book is dedicated to our families and friends for your unwavering love, support, and your understanding of our pursuit of our passions. Thank you for everything you do for us and for making our lives complete.

Dear Friend,

Thank you for purchasing our ***Celticology Trivia Challenge*** game book!

We hope you enjoy it as much as we enjoyed researching and putting it together. This book can be used over and over again in many different ways. One example would be to use it in a head-to-head challenge by alternating questions between Celtic basketball fans – or by playing as teams. Another option would be to simply challenge yourself to see how many questions you could answer correctly. No matter how you choose to use this book, you'll have fun and maybe even learn a fact or two about Celtics basketball.

We have made every attempt to verify the accuracy of the questions and answers contained in this book. However it is still possible that from time to time an error has been made by us or our researchers. In the event you find a question or answer that is questionable or inaccurate, we ask for your understanding and thank you for bringing it to our attention so that we may improve future editions of this book. Please email us at tprippey@trivianthology.com with those observations and comments.

Have fun playing ***Celticology Trivia Challenge***!

Paul & Tom

Paul Wilson & Tom Rippey
Co-Founders, Kick The Ball, Ltd

PS – You can discover more about all of our current trivia game books by visiting us online at www.TriviaGameBooks.com.

Table of Contents

How to Play

Celticology Trivia Challenge

Book Format:

There are four quarters, each made up of fifty questions. Each quarter's questions have assigned point values. Questions are designed to get progressively more difficult as you proceed through each quarter, as well as through the book itself. Most questions are in a four-option multiple-choice format so that you will at least have a 25% chance of getting a correct answer for some of the more challenging questions.

We've even added an *Overtime* section in the event of a tie, or just in case you want to keep playing a little longer.

Game Options:

One Player -
To play on your own, simply answer each of the questions in all the quarters, and in the overtime section, if you'd like. Use the *Player / Team Score Sheet* to record your answers and the quarter *Answer Keys* to check your answers. Calculate each quarter's points and the total for the game at the bottom of the *Player / Team Score Sheet* to determine your final score.

Two or More Players –
To play with multiple players decide if you will all be competing with each other individually, or if you will form and play as teams. Each player / team will then have its own *Player / Team Score Sheet* to record its answer. You can use the quarter *Answer Keys* to check your answers and to calculate your final scores.

The *Player / Team Score Sheets* have been designed so that each team can answer all questions or you can divide the questions up in any combination you would prefer. For example, you may want to alternate questions if two players are playing or answer every third question for three players, etc. In any case, simply record your response to your questions in the corresponding quarter and question number on the *Player / Team Score Sheet*.

A winner will be determined by multiplying the total number of correct answers for each quarter by the point value per quarter, then adding together the final total for all quarters combined. Play the game again and again by alternating the questions that your team is assigned so that you will answer a different set of questions each time you play.

You Create the Game -
There are countless other ways of using ***Celticology Trivia Challenge*** questions. It's limited only to your imagination. Examples might be using them at your tailgate or other professional basketball related party. Players / Teams who answer questions incorrectly may have to perform a required action, or winners may receive special prizes. Let us know what other games you come up with!

Have fun!

Preseason

1-Point Questions

1) How was the original nickname for the Boston Celtics chosen?

A) The first coach was Irish
B) The founder was Irish
C) Boston's large Irish population
D) The original team came from Ireland

2) What are the Celtics' team colors?

A) Green and Black
B) Green and White
C) Black, Green, and White
D) Green, White, Black, and Buff

3) What is the name of the arena where the Celtics play?

A) Fleet Center
B) TD Banknorth Garden
C) Sports Authority Garden
D) Conte Forum

4) How many Celtics players have been named NBA Sixth Man of the Year?

A) 2
B) 3
C) 5
D) 7

5) Which NBA Division do the Celtics play in?

A) Pacific
B) Central
C) Atlantic
D) Northwest

6) Which Celtic holds the team record for games played?

A) Larry Bird
B) Robert Parish
C) Kevin McHale
D) John Havlicek

7) The Celtics have made the NBA Playoffs 40 times.

A) True
B) False

8) Who has coached the most games for the Celtics?

A) Glenn "Doc" Rivers
B) Arnold "Red" Auerbach
C) K.C. Jones
D) Tom Heinsohn

9) Which state is former Celtics player Larry Bird from?

A) Illinois
B) Massachusetts
C) Kentucky
D) Indiana

10) The Celtics have had two foreign-born players who were also father and son.

A) True
B) False

11) How many NBA Championships have the Celtics won?

A) 9
B) 12
C) 17
D) 23

12) What object was found on the first Celtics logo?

A) Horseshoe
B) Four Leaf Clover
C) Shamrock
D) Leprechaun

13) Who was the first seven-footer to play for the Celtics?

A) Mel Counts
B) Charles Claxton
C) Stojko Vrankovic
D) Robert Parish

14) In what year was Arnold "Red" Auerbach enshrined into the Naismith Memorial Basketball Hall of Fame?

A) 1969
B) 1972
C) 1978
D) 1984

15) The seating capacity for Celtics' games at TD Banknorth Garden is greater than 20,000.

A) True
B) False

16) What year did the Celtics play their first game?

A) 1941
B) 1946
C) 1949
D) 1952

17) Which player led the Celtics in average points per game in the 2007-08 season?

A) Paul Pierce
B) Leon Powe
C) Kevin Garnett
D) Ray Allen

18) Against which Eastern Conference opponent do the Celtics have the most regular-season wins?

A) Philadelphia 76ers
B) Detroit Pistons
C) Atlanta Hawks
D) New York Knicks

19) Which team was the Celtics' first opponent at the Boston Garden?

A) Chicago Stags
B) Providence Steamrollers
C) New York Knicks
D) Toronto Huskies

20) Which of the following Celtics player has not won the NBA MVP Trophy?

A) Larry Bird
B) Bill Russell
C) Bob Cousy
D) All of the above have won

21) Did the Celtics make the playoffs their first season?

A) Yes
B) No

22) Which Celtic player is second in the league for both three-pointers attempted and made?

A) Ray Allen
B) Antoine Walker
C) Larry Bird
D) Bill Sharman

23) Which Celtics head coach had the most career wins?

A) K.C. Jones
B) Chris Ford
C) Red Auerbach
D) Bill Fitch

24) Which of the following Celtics head coaches had the worst playoff record?

A) John Russell
B) Chris Ford
C) Doc Rivers
D) Jim Rodgers

25) Which of the following Celtics players had fewer than ten career triple doubles?

A) Larry Bird
B) Paul Pierce
C) Antoine Walker
D) None of the Above

26) Which season did the Celtics first win 50 games?

A) 1947-48
B) 1951-52
C) 1956-57
D) 1964-65

27) What is the Boston record for most consecutive NBA Playoff appearances?

A) 7
B) 10
C) 13
D) 19

28) Did Larry Bird ever lead the NBA in free-throw percentage in a season as a player for the Celtics?

A) Yes
B) No

29) What was the name of the original league the Boston Celtics joined?

A) Basketball Association of America
B) National Basketball Association
C) National Basketball League
D) American Basketball Associations

30) Who led Boston in rebounds in the 2007-08 season?

A) Kendrick Perkins
B) Paul Pierce
C) Kevin Garnett
D) Rajon Rondo

31) Which team has Boston played the most in the NBA Playoffs?

A) Los Angeles Lakers
B) Philadelphia 76ers
C) New York Knicks
D) Atlanta Hawks

32) Against which team did the Celtics get their first-ever home victory?

A) Providence Steamrollers
B) Chicago Stag
C) Pittsburgh Ironmen
D) Toronto Huskies

33) Which player scored the most points in a single game against the Celtics?

A) Elgin Baylor
B) Michael Jordan
C) Kareem Adbul-Jabbar
D) Wilt Chamberlain

34) What year did the Boston Celtics win their first Eastern Conference Title?

A) 1951-52
B) 1964-65
C) 1973-74
D) 1978-79

35) Every player on the Celtics' roster had at least one block in the 2007-08 season.

A) True
B) False

36) How many times has a Celtics player led the league in free-throw percentage in a season?

A) 3
B) 7
C) 10
D) 13

37) Who holds the Celtics' record for most points scored in a single game?

A) Larry Bird
B) John Havlicek
C) Kevin Garnett
D) Todd Day

38) How many first round draft picks did the Boston Celtics have in 2001?

A) 1
B) 2
C) 3
D) 4

39) Who holds the Celtics' career record for blocked shots?

A) Larry Bird
B) Kevin McHale
C) Robert Parish
D) Paul Pierce

40) For which team was former Celtics player Larry Bird a coach?

A) Cleveland Cavaliers
B) Chicago Bulls
C) Detroit Pistons
D) Indiana Pacers

41) Which team holds the record for most points scored against the Celtics in a regular-season game?

A) Detroit Pistons
B) New York Knicks
C) New Jersey Nets
D) Philadelphia 76ers

42) What is the Celtics' record for consecutive winning seasons?

A) 7
B) 10
C) 14
D) 19

43) Which of the following Celtics players was not named NBA Rookie of the Year?

A) Larry Bird
B) Kevin Garnett
C) Dave Cowens
D) Tom Heinsohn

44) How many Atlantic Division Titles did the Celtics win under Red Auerbach?

A) 5
B) 8
C) 10
D) 14

45) What is the Boston record for most points scored in a playoff game?

A) 128
B) 135
C) 144
D) 157

46) How many times has Boston had two players named First Team All-NBA in the same season?

A) 3
B) 5
C) 8
D) 13

47) Have the Celtics ever had a player at least 40 years old?

A) Yes
B) No

48) Who holds the Celtics' all-time record for single season scoring average?

A) John Havlicek
B) Paul Pierce
C) Larry Bird
D) Antoine Walker

49) Who holds the Celtics' career record for points scored?

A) Larry Bird
B) Kevin McHale
C) Robert Parish
D) John Havlicek

50) In his sixteen years as Celtics head coach, how many losing seasons did Red Auerbach have?

A) 0
B) 1
C) 3
D) 5

Preseason Celtic Cool Fact

The Boston Celtics is a team of firsts. The Celtics were the first team in the NBA to average 100 points per game. During the 1954-55 season, they averaged 101.4 points per game. Another NBA first occurred in 1964. On December 26, Red Auerbach started the first all-black team. Those starters were K.C. Jones, Sam Jones, Willie Naulls, Satch Sanders, and Bill Russell. After Auerbach retired, he hired the NBA's first black coach, Bill Russell. He also hired K.C. Jones (another former black player) who ironically started an all-white team. The Celtics have yet another first for the league. Chris Ford scored the NBA's first three-point field goal on October 12, 1979 vs. Houston Rockets. The three-point field goal was established in 1979 by the NBA.

Preseason Answer Key

1) C – Boston's large Irish population (The founder wanted to attract the attention of as many people in Boston as possible. Other names considered were the Whirlwinds, Unicorns, and Olympics.)
2) D – Green, White, Black, and Buff
3) B – TD Banknorth Garden (The Celtics have played at this locale since 1995. It was known as the Fleet Center until 2005.)
4) A – 2 (Kevin McHale won the award in 1983-84 and 1984-85. Bill Walton won in 1985-86.)
5) C – Atlantic (The Celtics have been a part of the Atlantic Division since its formation in 1971.)
6) D – John Havlicek (1,270 games; He is ahead of Robert Parish by 164 games.)
7) A – True (The Celtics have played in the NBA playoffs 46 times. They have played a total of 524 playoff games.)
8) B – Arnold "Red" Auerbach (He coached for 16 consecutive seasons [1,340 games].)
9) D – Indiana (Bird grew up in a small southern-Indiana town called French Lick.)
10) B – False (They have never had a father and son both play on the team.)

11) C – 17 (1957, 1959-66, 1968, 1969, 1974, 1976, 1981, 1984, 1986, and 2008)

12) D – Leprechaun (The leprechaun logo was originally designed by Zang Auerbach, brother of former coach "Red" Auerbach, in the 1950. The logo has evolved in the last 50 years, with the most popular being the leprechaun traced in black wearing only green and black clothes.)

13) A – Mel Counts (He was the first 7'0" player to play for the Celtics. He was drafted in the first round in 1964.)

14) A – 1969 (Red Auerbach was an incredible coach, earning many honors, including seven honorary degrees from various schools. He was selected as coach of the 25th anniversary team in 1982.

15) B – False (TD Banknorth Garden has a seating capacity of 18,624.)

16) B – 1946 (Their first game was played on November 5th in front of only 4,329 fans.)

17) A – Paul Pierce (He scored an average of 19.6 points per game.)

18) D – New York Knicks (The Celtics have won 263 regular-season games vs. the Knicks.)

19) A – Chicago Stags (The game was delayed by an hour when the wooden backboard was damaged during warm-ups.)

20) D – All of the above have won (Cousy [1956-57], Russell [1957-58, 1960-63, & 1964-65], and Bird [1983-86]; Also Dave Cowens [1972-73])

21) B – No (The Celtics didn't make the playoffs until their second year as a team.)

22) A – Ray Allen (He has attempted 5,430 three-pointers and has made 2,155, second to Reggie Miller.)

23) C – Red Auerbach (He has a total of 885 career wins.)

24) D – Jim Rodgers (His winning percentage over two seasons is .250 in the playoffs [2-6].)

25) B – Paul Pierce (He has 6 career triple-doubles.)

26) C – 1956-57 (The Celtics won 44 regular-season games and 7 playoff games for 51 overall wins.)

27) D – 19 (The Celtics were in the Playoffs from 1951-69.)

28) A – Yes (4 seasons; 1983-84 [.888], 1985-86 [.896], 1986-87 [.910], and 1989-90 [.930])

29) A – Basketball Association of America (The Celtics joined the league in 1946. The BAA merged with the NBL in 1949 to form the NBA.)

30) C – Kevin Garnett (He had 655 total rebounds in the regular season and 274 in the playoffs.)

31) B – Philadelphia 76ers (The Celtics have played the 76ers a total of 93 times in the playoffs.)

32) D – Toronto Huskies (The Celtics won, 53-49, on November 16, 1946.)

33) A – Elgin Baylor (64 points at Minneapolis on November 8, 1959)

34) C – 1973-74 (The Celtics won the series against New York, 4-1. The NBA was not split into conferences until the 1970-71 season. The NBA had divisions prior to that season.)

35) B – False (Gabe Pruitt is the only team member without any blocks during the 2007-08 season.)

36) D – 13 (Bill Sharman [7 seasons], Larry Siegfried [2 seasons], and Larry Bird [4 seasons])

37) A – Larry Bird (60 points vs. Atlanta in 1985)

38) C – 3 (They drafted Joe Johnson, Kedrick Brown, and Joseph Forte.)

39) B – Kevin McHale (1,971 career blocks in 13 seasons)

40) D – Indiana Pacers (Bird coached the Pacers from 1997-00, leading them to the NBA Finals in 2000.)

41) A – Detroit Pistons (The Pistons scored 160 points in a 160-117 win over the Celtics on March 9, 1979.)

42) C – 14 (From 1955-56 to 1968-69)

43) B – Kevin Garnett (Heinsohn 1956-57; Cowens 1970-71; and Bird 1979-80)

44) C – 10 (Celtics won the Atlantic Division from 1956-57 to 1965-66 under Red Auerbach.)

45) D – 157 (During a home playoff game vs. New York on April 28, 1990)

46) C – 8 (The most notable season was 1958-59 when three players were named First Team [Bob Cousy, Bill Sharman, and Bill Russell].)

47) A – Yes (Robert Parish was 40 years old during his final season in 1993-94.)

48) C – Larry Bird (29.9 Points Per Game in 1987-88)

49) D – John Havlicek (26,395 career points)

50) B – 1 (39-40 record in 1954-55)

Note: All answers valid as of the end of the 2007-08 season, unless otherwise indicated in the question itself.

1) How many times has Boston won by more than 40 points?

A) 9
B) 12
C) 16
D) 21

2) What was the Celtics' highest team point total in a game in the 2007-08 season?

A) 119
B) 129
C) 134
D) 140

3) How many ex-Celtics players went on to become head coach of the Celtics?

A) 1
B) 3
C) 5
D) 7

4) Against which Western Conference opponent do the Celtics have the most wins during the regular season?

A) Golden State Warriors
B) Los Angeles Lakers
C) Detroit Pistons
D) Sacramento Kings

5) Who was the Celtics' first recorded team captain?

A) Bob Donham
B) Bob Cousy
C) Bill Russell
D) Chuck Cooper

6) Where did Doc Rivers coach before joining the Celtics?

A) Indiana Pacers
B) New York Knicks
C) San Antonio Spurs
D) Orlando Magic

7) Bill Russell individually holds the Celtics' records for rebounding in a single season, game, half, and quarter.

A) True
B) False

8) What is the Celtics' all-time largest margin of victory?

A) 45 points
B) 51 points
C) 59 points
D) 68 points

9) In what category did Celtics player Kevin McHale lead the NBA in the 1986-87 and 1987-88 seasons?

A) Assists
B) Field-Goal Percentage
C) Scoring
D) Free-Throw Percentage

10) What is the name of the cheerleading group that cheers on the Celtics at TD Banknorth Garden?

A) Shamrock Squad
B) Lucky Ladies Squad
C) Celtics Dancers
D) The Clover Girls

11) Who was the Celtics' first-ever draft pick?

A) Gene Stump
B) Saul Mariaschin
C) George Hauptfuehrer
D) Eddie Ehlers

12) What team has never played an overtime period against the Celtics?

A) San Antonio Spurs
B) Dallas Mavericks
C) Memphis Grizzlies
D) Phoenix Suns

13) Was Larry Bird ever named to the First Team NBA All-Defensive Team as a player for the Celtics?

A) Yes
B) No

14) Who is the shortest Celtics player to win the All-Star Weekend Slam-Dunk contest?

A) Gerald Green
B) Ricky Davis
C) Dee Brown
D) Greg Minor

15) What is the highest number ever worn by a Celtics player?

A) 66
B) 88
C) 96
D) 99

16) Which team handed the Boston Celtics their worst loss in franchise history?

A) Washington Wizards
B) Detroit Pistons
C) Portland Trail Blazers
D) Philadelphia 76ers

17) What was the Celtics' longest winning streak in the 2007-08 season?

A) 7 games
B) 10 games
C) 13 games
D) 17 games

18) When was the last season Boston won 60 or more games in the regular season?

A) 1987-88
B) 1990-91
C) 2001-02
D) 2007-08

19) What is the Boston record for most consecutive losses in a season?

A) 10 games
B) 13 games
C) 18 games
D) 24 games

20) How many all-time NBA Playoff games have the Celtics won?

A) 281
B) 304
C) 322
D) 335

21) The Celtics scored greater than 8,000 points as a team in the 2007-08 season.

A) True
B) False

22) Which season did the Celtics set their team records for three-pointers made and attempted?

A) 1987-88
B) 1989-90
C) 1997-98
D) 2002-03

23) How long was the Celtics' longest losing streak in the 2007-08 season?

A) 2 games
B) 3 games
C) 5 games
D) 7 games

24) How many times have Celtics players been named to the First Team NBA All-Defensive Team?

A) 5
B) 8
C) 11
D) 14

25) From which team was Celtics player Leon Powe traded in 2006?

A) Phoenix Suns
B) Denver Nuggets
C) Seattle Supersonics
D) Memphis Grizzlies

26) Which Celtics player has been named to the most All-NBA First or Second Teams combined?

A) Larry Bird
B) John Havlicek
C) Bob Cousy
D) Bill Russell

27) Which of the following coaches was not a Celtics assistant coach prior to becoming their head coach?

A) Rick Pitino
B) K.C. Jones
C) Jim Rodgers
D) Chris Ford

28) Nate Archibald and Paul Pierce are the only two Celtics to record 20 or more free throws made in a single game.

A) True
B) False

29) How many times have Celtics playoff games gone into overtime?

A) 26
B) 27
C) 31
D) 33

30) How many Celtics coaches never had a losing record for the regular season (minimum 3 seasons)?

A) 1
B) 3
C) 4
D) 6

31) How many times has a Celtics player been named NBA Player of the Week?

A) 21
B) 25
C) 32
D) 39

32) Which jersey number have the Celtics retired twice?

A) 18
B) 21
C) 24
D) 33

33) What is the Boston team record for most three-pointers made in a single game?

A) 12
B) 14
C) 17
D) 21

34) When was the last time a Celtics player recorded a triple double?

A) December 13, 2002
B) March 8, 2006
C) November 8, 2006
D) February 12, 2008

35) Did any ex-Celtics players, who became the team's head coach, have a winning coaching record?

A) Yes
B) No

36) What is the Celtics' record for field goals made in a regulation game?

A) 63
B) 67
C) 72
D) 80

37) Who was the first team the Celtics played in the new TD Banknorth Garden?

A) Minnesota Timberwolves
B) Milwaukee Bucks
C) Miami Heat
D) Chicago Bulls

38) What year did Boston first score 100+ points in a game?

A) 1949
B) 1950
C) 1951
D) 1953

39) Has any Celtics player ever recorded 10 or more steals in a single game?

A) Yes
B) No

40) What is the record for most points scored by the Celtics in a non-overtime regular-season game?

A) 164
B) 165
C) 168
D) 173

41) With which National Lacrosse League team will Boston share its home court?

A) Boston Blazers
B) Boston Brewers
C) Boston Bruins
D) Boston Bandits

42) What are the most three-pointers ever attempted by the Celtics in a single game?

A) 29
B) 33
C) 38
D) 41

43) Which of the following Celtics played fewer than 725 games for Boston?

A) Kevin Garnett
B) Paul Pierce
C) Dave Cowens
D) Tom Heinsohn

44) What is Boston's record for most consecutive Atlantic Division Titles?

A) 2
B) 5
C) 7
D) 9

45) Which Celtic scored the most points coming off the bench in the 2007-08 season?

A) Tony Allen
B) Sam Cassell
C) James Posey
D) Leon Powe

46) How many regular-season games did the Celtics sellout in 2007-08?

A) 35
B) 38
C) 40
D) All of their home games

47) Which Eastern Conference opponent has the most victories over the Celtics?

A) Detroit Pistons
B) Philadelphia 76ers
C) New York Knicks
D) Atlanta Hawks

48) On what street was the Old Garden located?

A) Staniford Street
B) Medford Street
C) Merrimac Street
D) Causeway Street

49) Robert Parish holds the Celtics' single-game Playoff record for most blocks vs. Philadelphia.

A) True
B) False

50) For which NBA team did Celtics Coach Doc Rivers most recently play?

A) Atlanta Hawks
B) New York Knicks
C) San Antonio Spurs
D) Orlando Magic

Regular Season Celtic Cool Fact

Who cares? The Boston Celtics care. The Celtics have given back to the Boston metropolitan area for many years. In the 2006-07 season alone, the Boston Celtics Shamrock Foundation donated 18,000 tickets to the community. They awarded 18,000 incentives to Boston Public Middle School students in promoting perfect attendance. That's not all. The Shamrock Foundation also awarded 22,800 incentives to area elementary school students to promote literacy. 250 appearances were made throughout the season by players, coaches, staff, and legendary figures. Plus, the team volunteered over 350 hours. They continue to improve on their community involvement. In September 2008, the Shamrock Foundation is hosting its first golf tournament to raise money so the Celtics can provide even more outreach and service to their community. These are just a couple of the examples how the Celtics are giving back.

Regular Season Answer Key

1) C – 16 (The most recent was against the New York Knicks, 104-59, on November 29, 2007.)
2) A – 119 (The Celtics beat the Grizzlies 119-89 and the Nuggets 119-93.)
3) D – 7 (Bill Russell [1966-69], Tom Heinsohn [1969-78], Thomas Sanders [1978-79], Dave Cowens [part of 1978-79], K.C. Jones [1983-88], Chris Ford [1990-95], and M.L. Carr [1995-97])
4) A – Golden State Warriors (The Celtics have an all-time record of 193-126 against the Warriors for a .605 winning percentage.)
5) B – Bob Cousy (He held this role from 1950-63.)
6) D – Orlando Magic (Rivers was the Magic coach from 1999-03.)
7) A – True (1,930 rebounds in a season; 51 in a game; 32 in a half; and 17 in a quarter)
8) B – 51 points (This happened against Philadelphia [153-102] on March 7, 1962.)
9) B – Field-Goal Percentage (He shot 790-1,307 [.604] in the 1986-87 season and 550-911 [.604] in the 1987-88 season.)
10) C – Celtics Dancers (The cheerleading squad is only in its third season. Twenty-one women from around the country were selected to be a part of this group.)

11) D – Eddie Ehlers (Round 1, Pick 1 in 1947 NBA Draft from Purdue.)

12) A – San Antonio Spurs (Every other team in the league has played at least one overtime game against the Celtics.)

13) B – No (Bird was selected for the Second NBA All-Defensive Team during 3 seasons [1981-83].)

14) C – Dee Brown (6'2"; Brown won in 1991, defeating Shawn Kemp in the finals.)

15) D – 99 (Worn by Roy Rogers, Jr. 1997-98)

16) B – Detroit Pistons (52 point loss, 66-118, on January 31, 2003)

17) B – 10 games (February 24, 2008-March 12, 2008; The Utah Jazz broke their winning streak, defeating the Celtics by 18 points on March 14 [92-110].)

18) D – 2007-08 (Their record was 66-16.)

19) C – 18 games (January 7, 2007-February 11, 2007; Losing streak ended vs. Milwaukee on February 14, 2007.)

20) B – 304 (They have won 204 home games and 100 away games.)

21) A – True (The team scored 8,245 total points.)

22) D – 2002-03 (719 three-pointers made and 1,994 attempted)

23) B – 3 games (February 19, 2008-February 22, 2008; The Celtics broke the streak by beating Portland on February 24 [112-102].))

24) D – 14 (Bill Russell [1968-69], Paul Silas [1974-76], John Havlicek [1971-76], Dave Cowens [1975-76], Kevin McHale [1985-88], Dennis Johnson [1986-87], and Kevin Garnett [2007-08])

25) B – Denver Nuggets (Powe entered the NBA Draft after his junior year of college and was picked 49th overall.)

26) C – Bob Cousy (He was named to the All-NBA 1st team for 10 consecutive years and to the 2nd team for the two following years for a total of 12 times.)

27) A – Rick Pitino (He was hired as head coach in 1997 and resigned mid-season 2000-01.)

28) A – True (Archibald made 20 free throws vs. Chicago on January 16, 1980 and Pierce made 20 at New York on November 2, 2002.)

29) C – 31 (16-15 overall, including a 5-6 2-OT record, [1] 3-OT and [1] 4-OT win)

30) C – 4 (Red Auerbach, Bill Russell, Bill Fitch, and K.C. Jones)

31) D – 39 (Larry Bird earned this honor 15 times.)

32) A – 18 (Jim Loscutoff requested that the number stay active for another player to wear. It was retired in honor of Dave Cowens in 1981.)

33) C – 17 (The Celtics made 17 three-pointers at Portland, January 3, 2003 and at Atlanta, November 17, 2001.)

34) C – November 8, 2006 (Ryan Gomes grabbed 12 rebounds, 10 assists, and scored 10 points against Charlotte.)

35) A – Yes (Bill Russell [.653], Tom Heinsohn [.616], Bill Fitch [.718], K.C. Jones [.729], and Chris Ford [.535])

36) C – 72 (Vs. Minneapolis on February 27, 1959)

37) B – Milwaukee Bucks (November 3, 1995; TD Banknorth Garden opened on September 30, 1995.)

38) A – 1949 (February 25, 1949; The Celtics beat St. Louis 102-83.)

39) B – No (The highest single game steal total is nine [Bird at Utah on February 18, 1985 and Pierce vs. Miami on December 3, 1999].)

40) D – 173 (Vs. Minneapolis on February 27, 1959)

41) A – Boston Blazers (They are an expansion team starting in January 2009.)

42) C – 38 (At Portland on February 13, 2003)

43) A – Kevin Garnett (He has only played for the Celtics for the 2007-08 season [71 games].)

44) B – 5 (1972-1976 and again from 1984-1988)

45) C – James Posey (545 points in the regular season)

46) D – All of their home games (41)

47) B – Philadelphia 76ers (The Celtics have lost to the 76ers a total of 218 times.)

48) D – Causeway Street (The old Boston Garden was located just feet away from the new TD Banknorth Garden.)

49) A – True (He had 7 blocks against Philadelphia in 1982.)

50) C – San Antonio Spurs (He retired from the league as a player in 1996 after 13 seasons. He scored a career 9,377 points.)

Note: All answers valid as of the end of the 2007-08 season, unless otherwise indicated in the question itself.

Conference Finals *3-Point Questions*

1) Which player scored the most points in a single game for the Celtics in the 2007-08 season?

A) Kevin Garnett
B) Rajon Rondo
C) Ray Allen
D) Paul Pierce

2) What is the Boston record for most overtime periods played in a single game?

A) 2
B) 3
C) 4
D) 5

3) Who is the only Celtics player to have scored 50+ points in two games?

A) Paul Pierce
B) Larry Bird
C) Kevin McHale
D) None of the Above

4) Which Celtic has had the most disqualifications [fouled out] in his career?

A) Tom Sanders
B) Larry Bird
C) Dave Cowens
D) Frank Ramsey

5) What is the Boston record for most consecutive home losses in a season at TD Banknorth Garden?

A) 7
B) 10
C) 13
D) 15

6) How tall was the shortest player to ever play for the Celtics?

A) 5'5"
B) 5'6"
C) 5'9"
D) 5'10"

7) The Celtics' first 100-point game occurred in the 1954-55 season.

A) True
B) False

8) Against which team do the Celtics have the most four-point plays?

A) Chicago Bulls
B) Detroit Pistons
C) Phoenix Suns
D) Los Angeles Lakers

9) In how many drafts has Boston not had a first round draft pick?

A) 2
B) 3
C) 5
D) 7

10) What is the Celtics' record for most consecutive NBA Playoff losses?

A) 3
B) 5
C) 7
D) 9

11) The Celtics enter the 2008-09 season with an all-time winning record in the regular season.

A) True
B) False

12) Which of the following players had more than one triple double as a Celtics player?

A) Robert Parish
B) Kevin Gamble
C) Dennis Johnson
D) None of the Above

13) Who was the leading scorer on the Celtics 2007-08 season roster?

A) Kevin Garnett
B) Rajon Rondo
C) Ray Allen
D) Paul Pierce

14) How many #1 overall NBA Draft picks has Boston had?

A) 0
B) 1
C) 3
D) 5

15) What is Boston's record for highest field-goal percentage in a single game during the NBA Playoffs?

A) .652
B) .657
C) .670
D) .693

16) What are the most losses by the Celtics to New York in one season?

A) 2
B) 3
C) 5
D) 6

17) What number did the Celtics retire in honor of Red Auerbach?

A) 00
B) 1
C) 2
D) 3

18) The Celtics have been eliminated in the first round of the NBA Playoffs as a one-seed from their division.

A) True
B) False

19) How many games did the Celtics sellout their first season in TD Banknorth Garden?

A) 8
B) 11
C) 19
D) 28

20) How many times has a Celtics' coach been named NBA Coach of the Year?

A) 3
B) 5
C) 6
D) 8

21) Against which team was the Celtics' last regular-season victory for the 2007-08 season?

A) Los Angeles Lakers
B) New York Knicks
C) New Jersey Nets
D) Atlanta Hawks

22) What is the record for most consecutive wins by Boston in the NBA Playoffs?

A) 5
B) 7
C) 9
D) 12

23) Which Western Conference opponent has the most all-time victories over the Celtics?

A) Golden State Warriors
B) Sacramento Kings
C) Los Angeles Lakers
D) Seattle Supersonics

24) What were the most games the Celtics played at home until the end of the 1966-67 season?

A) 28
B) 32
C) 36
D) 40

25) Which is the flagship station that broadcasts Boston Celtics games?

A) 850AM WEEI
B) 1030AM WBZ
C) 1150AM WTTT
D) 1510AM WWZN

26) How many times have the Celtics appeared in the NBA Finals?

A) 16
B) 17
C) 20
D) 22

27) Which player is not among the top five career leaders in three-point field goal percentage in Celtic history?

A) Larry Bird
B) Dana Barros
C) Danny Ainge
D) Paul Pierce

28) Who was the Celtics' first African-American player?

A) Chuck Cooper
B) Earl Lloyd
C) Hank DeZonie
D) Nat Clifton

29) In which decade were Celtics players named First Team All-NBA the most times?

A) 1940s
B) 1950s
C) 1970s
D) 1980s

30) How many seasons have the Celtics had fewer than five losses at home in the regular season?

A) 6
B) 7
C) 10
D) 12

31) Against which team do the Celtics have the most consecutive losses both at home and on the road?

A) Utah Jazz
B) Minneapolis Lakers
C) San Antonio Spurs
D) New York Knicks

32) The Celtics have an all-time winning record in game sevens of the NBA Playoffs.

A) True
B) False

33) What nickname was Larry Bird given by his first Celtics coach, Bill Fitch?

A) Flash
B) The Captain
C) Kodak
D) Larry Legend

34) Where did Coach Rivers play college basketball?

A) Indiana
B) Marquette
C) Michigan State
D) Boston College

35) Which team do the Celtics have the most wins against in the NBA Playoffs?

A) New York Knicks
B) Atlanta Hawks
C) Los Angeles Lakers
D) Philadelphia 76ers

36) Who was the last Celtics player (as a Celtic) to win a medal in the Olympic Games?

A) Paul Pierce
B) Larry Bird
C) Robert Parish
D) Kevin McHale

37) When was Boston's team record for blocked shots in the regular season set?

A) 1970-71
B) 1976-77
C) 1980-81
D) 1982-83

38) Who was the last Celtics player to score 50+ points in a game?

A) Paul Pierce
B) Kevin McHale
C) Larry Bird
D) Antoine Walker

39) Which player holds the Boston Celtics' rookie record for most points in a single game?

A) Bob Cousy
B) Bill Sharman
C) Bill Russell
D) Ed Macauley

40) Who were the only players to have 10 or more assists in a single game for Boston in the 2007-08 season?

A) Paul Pierce and Kevin Garnett
B) Kevin Garnett and Rajon Rondo
C) Kevin Garnett and Ray Allen
D) Paul Pierce and Rajon Rondo

41) Which player holds the Boston record for best field-goal percentage in a single regular season?

A) Kendrick Perkins
B) Cedric Maxwell
C) Bill Sharman
D) Antoine Walker

42) Which Western Conference opponent has Boston played the fewest number of times?

A) Dallas Mavericks
B) Minnesota Timberwolves
C) Memphis Grizzlies
D) Denver Nuggets

43) Who holds the Boston Celtics' franchise record for career assists?

A) Bob Cousy
B) Larry Bird
C) John Havlicek
D) Bill Russell

44) Who coached the Celtics in their first season?

A) Red Auerbach
B) Alvin "Doggie" Julian
C) John "Honey" Russell
D) Rick Pitino

45) Who was the last team the Celtics played in the Old Garden?

A) New York Knicks
B) Detroit Pistons
C) New Jersey Nets
D) Orlando Magic

46) What were the construction costs of the current Garden?

A) $153 million
B) $160 million
C) $174 million
D) $187 million

47) How many Celtics players scored over 1,000 points in the 2007-08 season?

A) 2
B) 3
C) 4
D) 6

48) What is the Celtics' longest drought between Eastern Conference Championships?

A) 13 years
B) 17 years
C) 20 years
D) 22 years

49) How many players have scored 15,000+ points during their career with the Celtics?

A) 2
B) 4
C) 7
D) 11

50) What is the Celtics' record for consecutive road wins in a season?

A) 8
B) 10
C) 11
D) 13

Conference Finals Celtic Cool Fact

On June 27, 1983, Dennis Johnson was traded to the Boston Celtics by the Phoenix Suns in exchange for former Celtic Rick Robey. This trade positively impacted the Celtics for the rest of the decade. He teamed up with Larry Bird, Kevin McHale, and Robert Parish to create an unstoppable team, winning NBA Championships in 1983-84 and 1985-86. Johnson made some great memories in his Celtic career, especially during the 1985 NBA Finals, where he made a series-tying jumper at the buzzer. He was named to the NBA All-Defensive First or Second Teams from 1983-87. Johnson may have ended his playing career with the Celtics in 1990, but remained a part of the Celtic family for four more years. He served as a scout from 1990-93. For the 1993-94 season, he served as assistant coach. What an impact this trade back in 1983 made on the Celtics. Dennis Johnson passed away in February 2007. He was a beloved part of the Celtic family and will be missed.

Conference Finals Answer Key

1) D – Paul Pierce (37 points at Seattle in a 104-96 win)
2) C – 4 (The Celtics won their only game to go to 4 OT periods against Philadelphia in the playoffs.)
3) B – Larry Bird (He scored 53 points vs. Indiana on March 30, 1983 and 60 points [career high] vs. Atlanta at New Orleans on March 12, 1985.)
4) A – Tom Sanders (He fouled out a total of 94 games and is ranked 3rd in personal fouls received [3,044].)
5) C – 13 (From December 20, 2006-February 9, 2007; The Celtics defeated Milwaukee on February 14 to end the streak.)
6) B – 5'6" (Mel Hirsch played only 13 games for the Celtics in 1946-47.)
7) B – False (Their first 100-point game was February 25, 1949 at home against St. Louis [102-83].)
8) D – Los Angeles Lakers (Two four-point plays: Scott Wedman on June 7, 1985 and Paul Pierce on March 2, 2005)
9) B – 3 (1979 [highest pick was the 3rd round], 1999 [their only pick was in the 2nd round], and 2002 [same as 1999 draft])

10) B – 5 (Against Detroit Pistons June 1, 1988-May 2, 1989; this streak spans over two seasons. The Celtics were defeated by the Pistons during Games 5 and 6 of the Eastern Conference Finals in 1988 and were swept [0-3] in the Eastern Conference First Round in 1989. The Celtics broke the streak by beating the New York Knicks in 1990.)
11) A – True (2,860-1,979 [.587])
12) D – None of the Above (Parish, Gamble, and Johnson each had 1 triple-double in their career.)
13) D – Paul Pierce (1,570 points)
14) B – 1 (Eddie Ehlers from Purdue in the 1947 draft)
15) C – .670 (The Celtics were 63-94 field goals vs. New York on April 28, 1990.)
16) D – 6 (Two different seasons: 1968-69 and 1970-71)
17) C – 2 (The ceremony occurred January 4, 19The number 2 was symbolic of Auerbach being the second most influential person in Celtics history.)
18) A – True (The Celtics were 1st in their division in 2004-05 and were eliminated in seven games by the Indiana Pacers.)
19) B – 11 (Average attendance during the 1995-96 season was 17,874.)
20) A – 3 (Red Auerbach [1964-65], Tom Heinsohn [1972-73], and Bill Fitch [1979-80])
21) C – New Jersey Nets (105-94 on April 16, 2008)

22) B – 7 (The Celtics earned this record against 3 teams in May 1989.)

23) C – Los Angeles Lakers (The Celtics have lost 144 total games to the Lakers.)

24) B – 32 (Due to playing on neutral courts, the Celtics did not play more than 32 home games until 1967-68 when they played 37.)

25) A – 850AM WEEI (This station has been the radio home for the Celtics since the beginning of the 2007-08 season.)

26) C – 20 (The Celtics played in the Finals 12 out of 13 years from 1957-69.)

27) D – Paul Pierce (He is ranked 8th on the all-time 3-point field-goal percentage list.)

28) A – Chuck Cooper (Celtics owner Walter Brown chose Cooper in the second round of the 1950 draft.)

29) B – 1950s (The Celtics had 17 players named to the All-NBA First Team during this decade.)

30) C – 10 (Their winningest season at home was in 1985-86 when they recorded 40 wins and only 1 loss.)

31) D – New York Knicks (11 losses at home [December 18, 1992-March 7, 1997] and 15 on the road [April 8, 1993-January 4, 2000]. The Knicks also have the record for consecutive victories overall against the Celtics [21 from April 8, 1993-January 19, 1998].)

32) A – True (The Celtics are 19-5 in Game 7s.)

33) C – Kodak (Bird had a way of capturing a mental image of every play on the court.)

34) B – Marquette (Rivers played from 1980-83, getting drafted after his junior season in the second round of the 1983 NBA Draft.)

35) D – Philadelphia 76ers (The Celtics have won 50 games over the 76ers during the playoffs.)

36) B – Larry Bird (He won a gold medal in the 1992 Olympics.)

37) C – 1980-81 (The Celtics recorded 594 blocks.)

38) A – Paul Pierce (50 points vs. Cleveland on February 15, 2006)

39) B – Bill Sharman (He scored 42 points on December 11, 1952.)

40) D – Paul Pierce and Rajon Rondo (Pierce – 3 games and Rondo – 10 games)

41) A – Kendrick Perkins (In 2007-08, he earned a .615 field-goal percentage [214-349].)

42) C – Memphis Grizzlies (They have played the Celtics 25 times.)

43) A – Bob Cousy (6,945 career assists)

44) C – John "Honey" Russell (He coached for 2 seasons [1946-48] with an overall record of 43-68.)

45) D – Orlando Magic (May 5, 1995; Celtics lost 92-95 and the Playoff series ended, 1-3.)

46) B – $160 million (The ground breaking was in May 1993 and the venue opened in the fall of 1995.)

47) B – 3 (Paul Pierce [1,570], Kevin Garnett [1,337], and Ray Allen [1,273])

48) C – 20 years (The Celtics did not win a Conference Championship from 1988-07.)

49) C – 7 (John Havlicek, Larry Bird, Robert Parish, Kevin McHale, Bob Cousy, Paul Pierce, and Sam Jones)

50) D – 13 (December 5, 1964-January 20, 1965; The streak ended with a loss at Philadelphia.)

Note: All answers valid as of the end of the 2007-08 season, unless otherwise indicated in the question itself.

1) How many teams have beaten the Celtics 10+ times during the regular season?

A) 1
B) 3
C) 4
D) None

2) How many times have the Celtics lost 60 or more games in one season?

A) 1
B) 2
C) 4
D) Never had a 60+ loss season

3) When was the last time Boston played on a neutral court?

A) 1968-69
B) 1973-74
C) 1987-88
D) 1999-00

4) Which NBA team did Celtics great Bill Sharman coach?

A) New York Knicks
B) Philadelphia 76ers
C) Chicago Bulls
D) Los Angeles Lakers

5) What is the most recent year the Celtics drafted two players from the same school?

A) 1974
B) 1978
C) 1985
D) 1987

6) Who holds the Celtics' record for steals in an NBA Playoff game?

A) Paul Pierce
B) Dennis Johnson
C) Rick Fox
D) Larry Bird

7) Who is the TV color analyst covering Celtics' games for the Fox Sports Network?

A) Cedric Maxwell
B) Willie Maye
C) Tom Heinsohn
D) Mike Gorman

8) Which Celtics head coach has the most career NBA Playoff victories?

A) Red Auerbach
B) Tom Heinsohn
C) Bill Russell
D) K.C. Jones

9) What is the Celtics' record for most consecutive sellouts at the Garden?

A) 647 games
B) 662 games
C) 677 games
D) 689 games

10) What is Boston's record for most team rebounds in a game?

A) 87
B) 96
C) 109
D) 114

11) What is the Celtics' team record for most points scored in a half?

A) 76
B) 80
C) 85
D) 91

12) What was the smallest average attendance to see the Celtics at the Old Garden?

A) 2,462
B) 3,608
C) 4,715
D) 5,096

13) What is the best finish for a Celtics player in the three-point shootout competition during All-Star Weekend?

A) 1st place
B) 2nd place
C) 3rd place
D) 4th place

14) Did the Celtics average greater than 100 points per game as a team in the 2007-08 season?

A) Yes
B) No

15) What number did Bob Cousy wear during his time at the Celtics?

A) 11
B) 14
C) 15
D) 17

16) Which team did the Celtics play on November 1, 1996 to open the 50th anniversary season?

A) Chicago Bulls
B) Milwaukee Bucks
C) New York Knicks
D) Philadelphia 76ers

17) Has there ever been a crowd smaller than 5,000 on hand to see the Celtics play at the current Garden?

A) Yes
B) No

18) How many NBA All-Star games have been played at the Garden?

A) 1
B) 2
C) 4
D) 5

19) What decade did the Celtics have the worst winning percentage in the regular season?

A) 1940s
B) 1950s
C) 1990s
D) 2000s

20) How many ex-Celtics players have a number retired in their honor?

A) 11
B) 15
C) 20
D) 23

21) Which of the following Celtics coaches was also the team's general manager?

A) Doc Rivers
B) Rick Pitino
C) Chris Ford
D) Red Auerbach

22) In what year did Danny Ainge lead the Celtics in minutes played?

A) 1984-85
B) 1985-86
C) 1986-87
D) 1987-88

23) What is the Boston record for most consecutive free throws made (over multiple games) by a single player?

A) 53
B) 60
C) 71
D) 97

24) What height is the tallest player to ever play for the Celtics?

A) 7'2"
B) 7'4"
C) 7'5"
D) 7'7"

25) Who did Boston draft in the first round of the 2008 NBA Draft?

A) Semih Erden
B) Gabe Pruitt
C) Jeff Green
D) J.R. Giddens

26) The Celtics have a better all-time regular season winning percentage versus the Eastern Conference than the Western Conference.

A) True
B) False

27) What is the Celtics' best improvement in total number of wins from one season to the next?

A) 28 wins
B) 31 wins
C) 38 wins
D) 42 wins

28) When was the last time every Celtics player scored in double figures in a single game?

A) 1956-57
B) 1959-60
C) 1962-63
D) 1965-66

29) Who holds the Celtics' record for most minutes played in their rookie season?

A) Dave Cowens
B) Kevin McHale
C) Paul Pierce
D) Antoine Walker

30) How many players, retired as a Celtic, (min. 5 seasons with Boston) are in the Basketball Hall of Fame?

A) 6
B) 7
C) 10
D) 13

31) Against which NBA Division did the Celtics have the best winning percentage in the 2007-08 season?

A) Atlantic
B) Central
C) Pacific
D) Southwest

32) How many times were Bob Cousy, Bill Sharman, and Bill Russell teammates on an NBA All-Star Team?

A) 1
B) 3
C) 4
D) 6

33) Which Celtics head coach coached the most NBA All-Star games?

A) Tom Heinsohn
B) K.C. Jones
C) Red Auerbach
D) Doc Rivers

34) Boston has had more players 7'0" or taller than players 5'11" or shorter.

A) True
B) False

35) How many seasons have the Celtics swept the Knicks during the regular season?

A) 5
B) 7
C) 10
D) 12

36) How many times have Celtics players won an Olympic medal for basketball (prior, during, or after their time at Boston)?

A) 7
B) 9
C) 12
D) 14

37) Which Celtics player played in the most Legends Games (held from 1984-1993)?

A) Larry Bird
B) Dave Cowens
C) Kevin McHale
D) John Havlicek

38) Who led the Celtics in three-point percentage in the 2007-08 season (min. 50 attempts)?

A) Sam Cassell
B) Paul Pierce
C) Ray Allen
D) Eddie House

39) Boston had a better winning percentage in the 2007-08 season after the All-Star break than before the break.

A) True
B) False

40) What decade did the Celtics have the best winning percentage in the regular season?

A) 1950s
B) 1960s
C) 1970s
D) 1980s

41) How many Celtics players (min. 5 seasons with Boston) are in the Naismith Hall of Fame?

A) 10
B) 14
C) 17
D) 19

42) How many teams have the Celtics beaten 10+ times during the regular season?

A) 1
B) 3
C) 4
D) None

43) What are the most points the Celtics have scored in a single quarter in the NBA Playoffs?

A) 39
B) 43
C) 46
D) 54

44) Who hit the final shot to give the Celtics the Game 7 win earning the Conference Finals Championship berth over Philadelphia in 1981?

A) Larry Bird
B) Kevin McHale
C) Robert Parish
D) Chris Ford

45) Which Celtics players have played in the most NBA All-Star games?

A) Bob Cousy and Larry Bird
B) Bob Cousy and John Havlicek
C) Larry Bird and Bill Russell
D) Bill Russell and John Havlicek

46) Who was the founder of the Celtics franchise?

A) Red Auerbach
B) John “Honey” Russell
C) Walter Brown
D) Alvin “Doggie” Julian

47) Which Celtic has the most Playoff career starts?

A) Robert Parish
B) Kevin McHale
C) Larry Bird
D) Dennis Johnson

48) How many Celtic players were selected as one of NBA’s 50 Greatest Players Team in 1996?

A) 8
B) 10
C) 12
D) 13

49) What was Celtics great Bob Cousy's nickname?

A) Houdini of the Court
B) The Smooth Cooz
C) Houdini of the Hardwoods
D) None of the Above

50) Which team did the USA Olympic team, with four future Celtics players, beat to win the gold in 2000?

A) Lithuania
B) Yugoslavia
C) Russia
D) France

Championship Finals Celtic Cool Fact

Danny Ainge, standout player for the Celtics, was not just a basketball player. Prior to being drafted by the Celtics in 1981, he played three seasons of baseball for the Toronto Blue Jays. During high school, Ainge was selected as First-Team All-American in football, basketball, and baseball. He was drafted by the amateur baseball draft in 1977 to Toronto. He earned his way to the major leagues in 1979 while still in college at Brigham Young (where he was playing basketball). After three years in the major league, he decided to go the basketball route. The Celtics bought out his contract from the Blue Jays who fought legal battles over the contract rights. Danny played 8 years for the Celtics (1981-89). Ainge made a significant impact, playing alongside Larry Bird, Kevin McHale, Dennis Johnson, and Robert Parish through the mid 1980s. Currently, he serves as Executive Director of Basketball Operations & General Manager for the Celtics, a role he has held since 2003.

Championship Finals Answer Key

1) D – None (The Celtics have played many teams 10+ times in a season, but none of them have beaten the Celtics in 10+ games.)
2) A – 1 (1996-97 under Coach M.L. Carr; 15-67 season record)
3) B – 1973-74 (The Celtics have a 9-2 record on neutral courts.)
4) D – Los Angeles Lakers (He coached them from the 1971-72 season to the 1975-76 season. The Lakers had a 6-16 record [.273] against the Celtics during his tenure.)
5) C – 1985 (The Celtics drafted two players from LaSalle: Albert Butts and Ralph Lewis.)
6) B – Dennis Johnson (He had 7 steals vs. Atlanta on April 29, 1986.)
7) C – Tom Heinsohn (He began his career as the Celtics' color analyst in 1981.)
8) A – Red Auerbach (90 career playoff wins)
9) B – 662 (The streak lasted from December 1980 through May 5, 1995 when the Celtics played Orlando in their final game at the Old Boston Garden.)
10) C – 109 (Vs. Detroit on December 24, 1960)

11) D – 91 (The Celtics set this record originally vs. Cincinnati on November 11, 1959 and tied the record vs. Detroit on February 10, 1960.)

12) B – 3,608 (In the Celtics' first season, 1946-47, their total annual game attendance was only 108,240 spread over 30 games.)

13) A – 1st Place (Larry Bird won the three-point shootout 3 consecutive years [1986-88] and is the only Celtic in history to win it.)

14) A – Yes (They averaged 100.5 points per game in the 2007-08 season.)

15) B – 14 (His jersey number retirement ceremony occurred on October 16, 1963.)

16) A – Chicago Bulls (The Celtics lost their home opener [98-107].)

17) B – No (The lowest attendance in the current Garden was 11,551 against Vancouver in the 2000-01 season.)

18) C – 4 (1951, 1952, 1957, and 1964; The East won all of the games hosted by Boston.)

19) A – 1940s (They recorded an 89-147 record during this decade for a .377 winning percentage.)

20) C – 20 (The most recent number-retiring ceremony was in 1998 for Robert Parish [00].)

21) D – Red Auerbach (He held the general manager position from 1967-84.)

22) D – 1987-88 (Ainge played in 81 games and played for 3,018 minutes.)
23) C – 71 (Larry Bird [December 19, 1989-February 13, 1990])
24) A – 7'2" (Artis Gilmore, Thomas Hamilton, Dwayne Schintzius, Bruno Sundov, and Stojko Vrankovic)
25) D – J.R. Giddens (Drafted from New Mexico [shooting guard], where he was named the Mountain West Conference Co-Player of the Year as a senior)
26) A – True (The Celtics have a .598 overall winning percentage against the Eastern Conference and a .596 against the Western Conference.)
27) D – 42 wins (The Celtics only had 24 wins in the 2006-07 season and improved to 66 wins in the 2007-08 season. This is an NBA record for best single season turnaround.)
28) D – 1965-66 (Vs. New York Knicks; Bill Russell 22, Tom Sanders 18, Sam Jones 16, Larry Siegfried 15, Mel Counts 13, Woodrow Saldsberry 13, Don Nelson 11, and K.C. Jones 10)
29) A – Dave Cowens (He played 3,076 minutes during his rookie season in 1970-71.)
30) C – 10 (Bob Cousy [1st retirement], Bill Russell, Bill Sharman, Frank Ramsey, John Havlicek, Sam Jones, Tom Heinsohn, K.C. Jones, Larry Bird, and Kevin McHale)

31) D – Southwest (The Celtics earned a .900 winning percentage [9-1] against teams in this division. Their only loss was at New Orleans Hornets [106-113] on March 22, 2008.)

32) B – 3 (They were teammates from 1958-1960.)

33) C – Red Auerbach (He served as head coach for 11 All-Star games [1957-67].)

34) A – True (There have been 25 Celtics players 7'0" or taller vs. 13 players 5'11" or shorter.)

35) B – 7 (1965-67, 1984-85, 1990-91, 2001-03, and 2007-08)

36) D – 14 (Clyde Lovellette won the first gold medal for a Celtic in 1952. Other Celtic Olympic-medal holders include: Bill Russell & K.C. Jones [1956]; Jim Barnes & Mel Counts [1964]; Jojo White & Charlie Scott [1968]; Joe Kleine [1984]; Larry Bird [1992]; Gary Payton [1996 and 2000]; and Ray Allen, Vin Baker & Kevin Garnett [2000].)

37) B – Dave Cowens (He was selected 8 consecutive years [1986-1993].)

38) C – Ray Allen (.398; Allen made 180 out of 452 three-point attempts.)

39) B – False (The Celtics had a .781 winning percentage after the break vs. .820 before the break.)

40) D – 1980s (.711 winning percentage [583-237])

41) B – 14 (Ed Macauley [1960], Bob Cousy [1970], Bill Russell [1974], Bill Sharman [1975], Frank Ramsey [1981], John Havlicek [1983], Sam Jones [1983], Tom Heinsohn [1986], K.C. Jones [1989], Nate Archibald [1991], Dave Cowens [1991], Larry Bird [1998], Kevin McHale [1999], and Robert Parish [2003])

42) B – 3 (Detroit Pistons [1964-65], New York Knicks [1963-64 and 1965-66], and Philadelphia 76ers [1963-64])

43) C – 46 (Vs. Detroit on March 24, 1968 and vs. St. Louis on March 27, 1960)

44) A – Larry Bird (He hit an 18-foot bank shot to take the lead and win the game, 91-90, despite being down by 11 points in the second half.)

45) B – Bob Cousy and John Havlicek (Both played in 13 NBA All-Star games, while Bill Russell and Larry Bird were selected for 12 games.)

46) C – Walter Brown (He founded the team in 1946 and owned the team until 1964. Brown also helped found the Basketball Association of America in 1946, which later merged with the National Basketball League to form the NBA in 1949. Brown died in 1964 and was inducted into the Hall of Fame in 1965.)

47) A – Robert Parish (168 career starts; Parish has 6 more starts than Larry Bird [162].)

48) D – 13 (Nate Archibald, Dave Bing, Larry Bird, Bob Cousy, Dave Cowens, John Havlicek, Sam Jones, Pete Maravich, Kevin McHale, Robert Parish, Bill Russell, Bill Sharman, and Bill Walton)

49) C – Houdini of the Hardwoods (Cousy introduced new ball-handling and passing, giving him this nickname. One of his other nicknames was "The Cooz".)

50) D – France (The four Celtics players contributing to the United States gold medal were Ran Allen, Vin Baker, Kevin Garnett, and Gary Payton. The U.S. ousted France, 85-75.)

Note: All answers valid as of the end of the 2007-08 season, unless otherwise indicated in the question itself.

Overtime Bonus *4-Point Questions*

1) Who was the youngest player to ever play for the Celtics?

A) Kendrick Perkins
B) Joseph Forte
C) Al Jefferson
D) Kedrick Brown

2) Which of the following Celtics coaches did not have a winning percentage higher than .500 in the NBA Playoffs?

A) Tom Heinsohn
B) Chris Ford
C) K.C. Jones
D) Bill Fitch

3) How many Celtics players had greater than 100 turnovers in the 2007-08 season?

A) 2
B) 3
C) 5
D) 6

4) Has any Celtics coach become an assistant coach after being a head coach?

A) Yes
B) No

5) Which Celtic has won the most All-Star Game MVP awards?

A) Larry Bird
B) Bill Russell
C) Nate Archibald
D) Bob Cousy

6) What college did ex-Celtics player Kevin McHale attend?

A) Minnesota
B) Michigan
C) Connecticut
D) North Carolina

7) The Celtics had the best record in the NBA in 1985-86.

A) True
B) False

8) How many times have the Celtics been swept in the NBA Playoffs?

A) 2
B) 3
C) 5
D) 6

9) What season was the Celtics' lowest attendance record set at the current Garden?

A) 2001-02
B) 2002-03
C) 2003-04
D) 2004-05

10) How many total banners do the Celtics have hanging from the rafters?

A) 61
B) 69
C) 76
D) 81

Overtime Bonus Answer Key

1) A – Kendrick Perkins (He was still 18 years old at the beginning of the 2003-04 season.)
2) B – Chris Ford (.448 winning percentage in the playoffs [13-16])
3) D – 6 (Paul Pierce [221], Rajon Rondo [147], Kevin Garnett [138], Ray Allen [127], Kendrick Perkins [125], and Tony Allen [109])
4) B – No (No Celtics coach in history has become assistant coach after being head coach.)
5) D – Bob Cousy (1954 and 1957)
6) A – Minnesota (McHale was drafted 3rd overall in 1980 by the Celtics.)
7) A – True (The Celtics were 67-15 and NBA Champions.)
8) D – 6 (1950-51, 1953-54, 1982-83, 1988-89, 2002-03, and 2003-04)
9) C – 2003-04 (Only 12,478 were in attendance at the game against Memphis on December 1, 2003.)
10) D – 81 (26 Division, 18 Regular Season, 20 Conference, and 17 League Titles)

Note: All answers valid as of the end of the 2007-08 season, unless otherwise indicated in the question itself.

Player / Team Score Sheet

CELTICOLOGY TRIVIA CHALLENGE

Name:____

Preseason				Regular Season				Conference Finals				Championship Finals				Overtime Bonus	
1		26		1		26		1		26		1		26		1	
2		27		2		27		2		27		2		27		2	
3		28		3		28		3		28		3		28		3	
4		29		4		29		4		29		4		29		4	
5		30		5		30		5		30		5		30		5	
6		31		6		31		6		31		6		31		6	
7		32		7		32		7		32		7		32		7	
8		33		8		33		8		33		8		33		8	
9		34		9		34		9		34		9		34		9	
10		35		10		35		10		35		10		35		10	
11		36		11		36		11		36		11		36			
12		37		12		37		12		37		12		37			
13		38		13		38		13		38		13		38			
14		39		14		39		14		39		14		39			
15		40		15		40		15		40		15		40			
16		41		16		41		16		41		16		41			
17		42		17		42		17		42		17		42			
18		43		18		43		18		43		18		43			
19		44		19		44		19		44		19		44			
20		45		20		45		20		45		20		45			
21		46		21		46		21		46		21		46			
22		47		22		47		22		47		22		47			
23		48		23		48		23		48		23		48			
24		49		24		49		24		49		24		49			
25		50		25		50		25		50		25		50			
___x 1 =___				___x 2 =___				___x 3 =___				___x 4 =___				___x 4 =___	

Multiply total number correct by point value/quarter to calculate totals for each quarter.

Add total of all quarters below.

Total Points:________

Thank you for playing Celticology Trivia Challenge.

Additional score sheets are available at:

www.TriviaGameBooks.com

Player / Team Score Sheet

Celticology Trivia Challenge

Name:____________________________________

Preseason				Regular Season				Conference Finals				Championship Finals				Overtime Bonus	
1		26		1		26		1		26		1		26		1	
2		27		2		27		2		27		2		27		2	
3		28		3		28		3		28		3		28		3	
4		29		4		29		4		29		4		29		4	
5		30		5		30		5		30		5		30		5	
6		31		6		31		6		31		6		31		6	
7		32		7		32		7		32		7		32		7	
8		33		8		33		8		33		8		33		8	
9		34		9		34		9		34		9		34		9	
10		35		10		35		10		35		10		35		10	
11		36		11		36		11		36		11		36			
12		37		12		37		12		37		12		37			
13		38		13		38		13		38		13		38			
14		39		14		39		14		39		14		39			
15		40		15		40		15		40		15		40			
16		41		16		41		16		41		16		41			
17		42		17		42		17		42		17		42			
18		43		18		43		18		43		18		43			
19		44		19		44		19		44		19		44			
20		45		20		45		20		45		20		45			
21		46		21		46		21		46		21		46			
22		47		22		47		22		47		22		47			
23		48		23		48		23		48		23		48			
24		49		24		49		24		49		24		49			
25		50		25		50		25		50		25		50			
__x 1 =___				__x 2 =___				__x 3 =___				__x 4 =___				__x 4 =___	

Multiply total number correct by point value/quarter to calculate totals for each quarter.

Add total of all quarters below.

Total Points:_______

Thank you for playing Celticology Trivia Challenge.

Additional score sheets are available at:

www.TriviaGameBooks.com